"The hero and the coward both feel the same thing, but the hero uses his fear, projects it onto his opponent, while the coward runs. It's the same thing, fear, but it's what you do with it that matters."

—Cus D'Amato

"Once that bell rings you're on your own. It's just you and the other guy."

—Joe Louis

HANDS UP!

It's Not Just About BOXING
It's About CHANGING YOUR LIFE!

John Mariotti with
John & Tim Sullivan

Publisher: The Enterprise Group, Powell, OH 43065

HANDS UP!

It's Not Just About Boxing—
It's About Changing Your Life!

Disclaimer: This book provides general information that is intended to inform and educate the reader on a general basis. Every effort has been made to assure that the information contained herein is accurate and timely as of the date of publication. However, it is provided for the convenience of the reader only.

The author, publisher and all affiliated parties expressly disclaim any and all express or implied warranties, including the implied warranty of merchantability and fitness for a particular purpose. Reliance on all information in this book is at the reader's sole risk.

The information presented herein may not be suitable for each reader's particular situation. It is recommended that each reader consult a professional in the reader's respective area of interest for further advice on this subject. Readers must be aware that boxing as a sporting activity has inherent risks of injury, and nothing in this book is intended to mitigate or reduce that risk. Any reader pursuing the activities described in this book does so solely at their own risk.

In no event are the Author, Publisher or any affiliated

party liable for any direct, indirect, incidental, consequential, or other damages of any kind whatsoever including lost profits, relative to the information or advice provided herein. Reference to any specific commercial product, process or service, are informational and do not constitute an endorsement or recommendation.

HANDS UP!

It's Not Just About Boxing
It's About Changing Your Life
FOREWORD

When you start to write a book, you are telling a story. This one is a story about two guys from Columbus, OH who decided to try living their idea, and fulfilling their dream—to own and operate their own boxing gym.

But they didn't just want to do it the old way. Neither did they want to become one of the "cookie-cutter" franchise gyms that are opening all over. This was going to be "personal," because boxing was personal, and the preparation needed, is something that each person does differently.

The Sullivan brothers also wanted their gym to appeal to all ages, both genders—in other words—everyone. The reason is simple. The most important lessons in boxing apply equally to life, and that's what this little book is all about. It's not just about boxing; it's about changing your life!

John Mariotti, Powell, OH 2013

INTRODUCTION

"Many people fail not so much because of their mistakes; they fail because they are afraid to try."
-- George Foreman

INTRODUCTION

When John and Tim Sullivan were growing up in the 1950's and 60's on the East Side of Columbus, OH, they never dreamed that they'd be the owner-operators of a boxing gym bearing their name. They certainly couldn't have imagined that they'd be the co-authors of a book like this either.

One thing they found as they grew up was that boxing was an ever-present part of their lives. Sure, they had "regular lives" too. Tim spent a stint in the Marines and then worked for Anheuser-Busch for over 30 years, before the entrepreneurial bug bit him. But he started boxing when he was 16 years old, and has been involved with it for most of his adult life.

John served his country in the Army, and then spent much of his adult life as a police officer—a decorated one at that—where he learned some of life's tougher lessons. He learned to box at an early age, and then developed those skills during a short career first as an amateur, then briefly as a professional boxer. He also participated in "Toughman" contests, placing in the Top 5 of a US/Canada competition. Tim supported him as a "corner-man" through it all.

While John was a police officer, he frequently assisted as a boxing coach at the Police Academy, teaching recruits boxing and self defense skills. As time went on, other police officers who knew of John's skills asked if he would help them and "teach them," or "show them a few things." One day John suggested that Tim come in with him, because Tim had a love for and knowledge of boxing too.

Soon they found plenty to do helping police officers learn the skills of boxing and hand-to-hand battles they might encounter in the course of apprehending criminals or just controlling rowdies. It was then that Tim observed to John that they (he) might get in trouble since he (Tim) was not an employee of the police department and had no legal basis for even being there, let alone "helping out."

It was then that John suggested, "Why don't we start our own boxing gym?" Early on, the two brothers never imagined that they would earn their livelihood in their senior years from their love of, and experience in the "sweet science"—as boxing is sometimes known. Yet, in both brothers' words, "we've been around boxing 'forever'!"

That's why, after his early retirement, in 2008 Tim and John decided to pursue John's suggestion and open their own gym. The hard job of starting a business began. First was the planning.

Getting Started—A Different Kind of Challenge

Tim had always been an entrepreneur at heart—although he'd had few ways to pursue this drive. Now the two Sullivan brothers had a mission: to open their own gym and operate a different kind of boxing gym.

Tim describes it very well. "Most boxing gyms struggle because they are "old-style" boxing gyms that service dedicated fighters. Since many of these fighters come from tough, inner city or low income backgrounds, there is never much money to pay for anything, least of all a gym. The 'old style gyms' are easily identified by the location (usually in a 'low-rent district'), the blood stains that mark the ring (boxing can be a brutal sport) and the clientele, tough, rough and tumble guys, who either have fought for things all of their lives, or young men who want to fight as an outlet for their aggression—and because it is something they are good at doing."

"These "old-style" boxing gyms always seem to struggle financially and many of them go under and close unless they can find a wealthy "patriarch" or become affiliated with some club or civic organization to help support them. Since we didn't have any of those, we concluded that we had better take a different approach. Plus our location was not typical of where you'd find old-style boxing gyms, or their clientele anyway."

"We wanted to open our gym in Powell, OH, an upscale and rapidly growing suburb of Columbus—not exactly the typical location for a boxing gym in early 2008. John and I spent hours at Frisch's talking and planning, thinking through how the gym would work, what we'd need to start it, including how much money it would take. I was willing to raid my IRA for the startup money, which we guessed would be about $40,000! I hoped I could get it back once the gym got going. It turned out that wasn't so easy."

The Beginning & Inspiration

When they opened the first version of Sullivan Brothers Gym in 2008, it may very well have been the only or first suburban gym of its kind in the area. Tim learned that it was no picnic doing a small business startup in the face of the worst recession in the US in modern history.

"We figured out that we had to make this a different kind of boxing gym—one that would appeal to whatever kind of clientele we could attract: women, kids, after-work professionals or executives, retirees, whoever wanted to come, get a good workout and learn the techniques of boxing. Many of these people had little interest in the 'old-style" boxing gym and didn't want to get in the ring and get bloodied and beat-up."

He smiles as he recounts his inspiration for the gym's idea: George Foreman—but not the tough, scowling brutal George of his early career—the smiling, happy, friendly George of his second career, the namesake of the Lean Mean Grilling Machine™ and TV commercials.

When Tim related this inspiration it became very clear. "In the ring, George Foreman was a killer, a huge, brutal fighter who knocked out nearly everyone he faced in the first part of his career, including great champs like Joe Frazier—who was knocked out by George in just two rounds. "

14

Foreman was an Olympic heavyweight champion and went undefeated in his first 40 pro fights, knocking out 90% of his opponents. After his loss to an aging Muhammad Ali in the "Rumble in the Jungle," and a series of other, less notable fights, that ultimately led to him losing the heavyweight championship, George Foreman "retired" to pursue life as a father (11 kids, five of them boys named George), and a minister.

When George Foreman came back into the public eye, he was quite different, less angry, and more at peace with himself and the world. He made a comeback as a fighter, and eventually re-captured the heavyweight championship at age 45 by knocking out Michael Moorer in the fourth round, and became the oldest ever to hold this crown. However, the new George, outside the ring, was jovial, smiling, inviting, and welcoming. The way Tim put it, "The new George was 'happy George,' and the public loved him."

Foreman followed his boxing career with a career as an entrepreneur and licensed his the name and image for use on the hugely successful George Foreman Lean Mean Fat-Grilling Machine—a small tabletop, electric grill—one of the most successful appliances ever.

The Start-up Challenges—"Early Rounds"

Tim and John figured that there was no reason Sullivan's Boxing Gym couldn't be a "friendly place" where you could either learn serious boxing, or get in shape using typical boxing-inspired workouts, or a little of both. They might get some serious boxers too, but that would be a bonus—and they needed far more than the "serious boxers" to make a go of it. Then, like all start ups, things didn't go quite as planned.

Here's how Tim describes it. "When the gym was in the planning phases, the vocal support of friends and acquaintances was terrific. Everyone we talked to told us they'd come to the gym and/or join it. We were really happy and optimistic. When we opened in a small space next to a popular store that gave music lessons and had lots of traffic. We were excited. Then a small handful of people showed up—not nearly the crowd we'd expected. That was in April 2008."

"We made all the typical mistakes. We bought too much 'stuff,' thinking we could sell it, but it didn't sell. We didn't know what all we needed in the way of equipment, because we had no idea how many people would be working out at one time. It was tough. John was still working as a police officer then, so sometime it was 'just me.' I did whatever was necessary: boxing coach, trainer, workout leader, janitor, business manager, and anything else to keep the doors open and the place operating."

When John retired in 2012, he joined Tim to help share the load and try to grow the boxing gym business. The gym moved to larger, more spacious quarters still across the street from the old location, out in the growing section of Powell between Old Sawmill Road and "new" Sawmill Road, the main north-south thoroughfare through Powell and Liberty Township.

Tim tells it this way, "We knew we had to find different ways to publicize the gym and get customers to come in and try it. That was a whole new learning process in itself. Fortunately we got a nice write up in one of the local Powell/Olentangy papers, which helped. We knew we had to be flexible while we found what would appeal to the general public, to get them into the gym to try it out.

We are still trying different things to see which of the various ideas work best, when, and what kind of people we attract—who are happy with their visits to the gym and keep coming back. We know we need to be more than just a gym that people come to and figure out what to do. Those are all over the place. We offer a different experience completely—and a great workout in the process."

Sayings from the Gym: "Let's have some fun!"

A NOTE from Tim and John: "Throughout this little book, we'll share some 'Stories from the Gym' so you can imagine the amazing, interesting, inspiring and sometimes humorous things that happened at Sullivan Brothers Gym."

John Mariotti: "How I Found the Sullivan Brothers."

This brings us to how I met John and Tim Sullivan and how/why we decided to do this book. I had passed the gym driving through the area on many occasions and was intrigued by the big sign on the beige building that simply said: **BOXING**.

Then I found an offer from Living Social in my email, offering an introductory set of lessons at an attractive price. Like most semi-retired, former business people, my life was becoming a bit too sedentary. I had been an athlete through most of my youth up until my 40's when my knees suggested I quit basketball and softball, played tennis until my early 60's when plantar fasciitis stopped that. Of course I have a bunch of exercise equipment in my basement, but that's too easy, and after a while, it gets boring too.

I've tried joining ordinary health clubs and/or gyms but treadmills, ellipticals, and exercise bikes are boring, and the contraptions called exercise machines seem to require knowledge of how to adjust them, how to use them, and a whole series of them to work on the various body parts.

But, for some inexplicable reason, I've enjoyed watching boxing for years. I realized that I knew a lot from the TV expert commentary, but nothing from a first hand basis, so I took the email offer, and stopped into Sullivan Brothers Boxing Gym. After a brief talk with Tim, I thought I might really enjoy the place and the people—and get a good workout while I learned how to box.

As soon as I had a couple of travel-free weeks, I signed up for boxing lessons at the young age of 71. I hoped it would help me stay fit and I knew I hated walking on a treadmill. In fact, the sign prominently displayed in their window says, *"No Boring Treadmills"*—my sentiment exactly!

Having the owners be a bit older appealed to me, since they were willing to make a few "training concessions," to help me avoid any unnecessary wear and tear on my aging (but still original equipment) knees. For example, I just can't handle jumping rope—or rather my knees can't, so I warm up differently—moving about the ring in a boxing stance with light hand weights and sort of "shadow boxing."

I found that the other person I met was Andre Wolf, who was, at 25 a fraction of my age. Andre was my "instructor" for my first session at the gym. A lot depends on having a good first experience, which makes you want to come back. Fortunately, Andre was a very engaging, helpful and knowledgeable young man, and, as I quickly learned, knew a lot about boxing (and kick boxing as well).

After just a few sessions, I bought some hand wraps of my own (a necessary item—but also a small commitment to sticking with it), and soon thereafter, my own boxing gloves—a bigger commitment, but still quite economical (initially the gym furnished each of these.) Now I was "into it."

After about 8-9 lessons I found that several things were happening. The training they used was definitely helping me get in shape—and it was far more interesting than treadmills, exercise bicycles, etc. I wasn't actually losing any weight, but my body shape was changing, and I was feeling better too. And, what was the most fun, I was learning the fundamentals of boxing too.

However, since I spent my career in the world of business— 30+ years as a professional, a manager, and an executive and then the past 20 as a board member, consultant, speaker and writer, I began to see many similarities between the lessons of boxing and the lessons of business—and life.

In living this kind of career for 50 years, I discovered that many of the things we learn (good and bad) actually applied in a wide variety of settings. The more I thought about it, the more I saw numerous lessons from the boxing gym/ring that translated to the world of business and to life in general. That's what triggered my interest in doing this book.

When I talked to John and Tim about the idea of a book, they liked it, and what they told me reinforced my experiences, including the phrase that became the subtitle of this book: **It's Not Just About Boxing—It's About Changing Your Life,** (The book's cover icon— a sign prominently displayed on the wall of the Sullivan Brothers Gym.)

Then a funny thing happened. The more we talked, we kept finding more and more lessons and examples in which boxing either provided a valuable life lesson, an important lesson about business/work—or both. One of the most interesting aspects of working with and then developing this book with Tim and John, (and also with Andre), was hearing and listing the *"Sayings from the Gym."*

These are things that one or both of them say so often, that they become almost the continuing mantras of learning about boxing—and about life—including the one phrase I heard more and more: "HANDS UP!" I was surprised to learn that of all the aspects of boxing I learned, one of the hardest things to do was the keep my "hands up."

Sayings from the Gym: "Hands up!"

These sayings you hear around the gym will be liberally scattered through the book, so you can get he feeling of hearing one of the two Sullivan brothers voices ring out over the thump of people hitting the heavy bags and the rapid staccato of several different people on the speed bags.

THE
FUNDAMENTALS

Without the fundamentals, the details are useless.

—*Vince Lombardi*

1

THE FUNDAMENTALS

The book that follows is organized into twelve chapters, just as championship boxing matches consist of twelve rounds of boxing. We hope to share many useful lessons we have learned, from our collective and yet very different backgrounds, and from the different people of all ages, sizes, shapes and genders, who come to the gym to learn about boxing and leave having learned a whole lot more.

We hope you enjoy this book and have as much fun reading it as we had putting it together. OK, there's the "bell," so it's time to get started.

There are many principles that are transferable from the "sweet science" of boxing, to the everyday world of work, business, and life. The 12 chapters that follow, like the 12 rounds of a championship fight, will describe the most important lessons to be learned, about boxing, work/business, and life. Let's get started where it all starts.

Balance

Balance is a critical part of life and it is imperative in boxing. In life, balance means finding the right mixture of your roles as a person, a family member, a professional or employee, a member of a community and a role model. The connotation of balance in boxing is a bit different.

If you lose your balance and go down to the canvas (the floor of the boxing ring), and if it happens as a result of a punch, that's called a knockdown—and it counts against you on a scorecard that will determine who wins the match. You must also get up within 10 seconds as the referee stands over you and counts up to ten.

This is where the life lesson comes into play. During your life, you will get "knocked down" figuratively if not literally, a lot of times. What matters is that you get back up and regain your balance. This getting up isn't always easy—but it is always critically important. In life, getting back up (regaining your balance) allows you to continue on—and that's very much like boxing—if you don't get up in 10 seconds, the match is over and you lose!

If you lose your balance in life or work the parts that usually suffer are family, loved ones, and your own personal condition. This is a different kind of "balance" from the physical balance needed in boxing—and yet it isn't very different at all—losing your feet in boxing or losing your perspective on what's important in life both result in the same thing.

You are down, "on the canvas" and you need to gather your wits about you and get up, and then do different, better things, or you'll be right back down there. To understand more about doing those different, and better things, we will tell you about them. Our lessons will bounce back and forth between boxing, work/business, and life because they are all very much alike in so many ways. Ready?

Sayings from the Gym: "You CAN DO it!"

Get in Shape—"Fighting Shape"

What allows you go be good at boxing is that first of all, you must be in "shape." By "shape" we mean good physical condition, which for boxing (and life) means a combination of **strength, flexibility and endurance.**

There are also different ways to interpret "getting in shape." There is "walking around shape," and "fighting shape," and these are very, very different. Walking around shape means generally pretty good physical condition that might come from the occasional workout, running or walking for exercise, doing moderate amounts of exercise either at home or on a treadmill at a workout facility.

Doing this puts you in decent physical shape—but in no way does it prepare you for the intensity of true competition—the physical confrontation. That's what we call "fighting shape." Fighting shape means building up your body in specific ways to be ready to do what's needed in "competition"—in this case a boxing match.

This is different than a body builder creates. It also includes building the strength and the flexibility to move into different positions as quickly as you must. However neither of these counts for much if you "run out of gas," so let's cover that topic first.

Sayings from the Gym: "Take a break! Get a drink."

(Fighting shape builds in bursts, so breaks are important
chances to recover.)

Endurance

First comes endurance. This may be the most important of the three. It is this endurance, when combined with perseverance that usually determines success. You can see this every day in boxing matches. As the fight wears on, it tires out both fighters. So do life—and work. Often it becomes clear who was better prepared—in better fighting shape—in terms of endurance. Then, when the match comes down to the tough times, perseverance shows—provided the fighter has the endurance to execute what needs to be done.

Either one alone is insufficient. In fact, it takes being in fighting shape, having the physical endurance to continue to perform and the mental toughness to persevere when you are "tired and beaten up." Both boxing and life causes you to become "tired and beaten up." How you handle it will determine how happy you will be with the outcome. Get in shape—"fighting shape"—and hang in there when the going gets tough. You'll win more often than lose.

Sayings from the Gym: "Get in shape—'fighting shape'—not just 'walking around shape'!"

Flexibility

Life changes constantly. So does a boxing match. Flexibility to "roll with a punch" (turning with it to reduce the impact) is just as important in work and life as it is in the ring. The ability to move, to adjust, to "evade," and then to "attack" is as important in life and work as it is in the boxing ring especially when trying to reduce the impact of a punch and recover from it. The only differences are in the specific meaning and interpretation of the words "evade" and "attack."

Attack in boxing usually means throwing punches. Attack in business usually means going after some business (or a job) that is held by someone else. Attack in life might mean making a determined commitment to do more, to do better and to accomplish something that had previously been hard to achieve—like helping a spouse, connecting with a child, leading a civic or church organization or, maybe, just getting a better handle on what you are doing with your time, effort and attention.

What matters most?   Attacking life and work means concentrating on what matters most—and that is constantly evolving.   But that is where the strength and flexibility is important in both boxing and in life.

Stories from the Gym: "The Tires Got Me!"

One series of exercises done at the gym involves tires—of all sizes and shape—truck tires, car tires, etc. Sometimes people beat on the large tires with sledgehammers. At other times, the weight of the tire is used in a different way. A common exercise involves a strap (harness) used to pull the tire around the parking area alongside the gym. First you pull the tire moving forward then you reverse the straps and "back-pedal" going backwards.

Like all exercises we try to make them as safe as possible to avoid injuries. Unfortunately, the "friction," when the tire drags changes, making it easier or harder to pull, so it's possible to stumble. In boxing, injuries to the hands usually come from hitting something. In this case the tire did it! It tripped up a lady and she hurt her hand (broke a bone) trying to break her fall. Nobody said boxing—or life—could be made "risk free!"

Strength

Make no mistake about it, strength is important in boxing. But as noted earlier, it is a specific sort of strength. Body builders build muscles, but often they are so bulked up that they lack the speed, flexibility and agility needed in boxing.

That means the strength training for boxing must accommodate all three of those factors—speed, flexibility and agility— and combine them with endurance. A round— three minutes of boxing can seem like an eternity. There is no escape from the ring, and depending on the kind of opponent, there may also be no escape from him/her.

A common misconception about strength in boxing is that it all depends on the upper body and arms. That's not true. Sure, strong arms and shoulders and chest and torso are important—as much to withstand punches as to deliver them. But the true power comes, as it does in most sports, from the coiling and uncoiling of the body from the legs upward through the "core" (abdomen to over-simplify it).

A strong core is what creates so much of the strength of truly powerful boxers. Then the flexibility and agility allow the strength in that core to be transmitted through the shoulder and arms to deliver (or defend against) punches.

Body action is important in virtually every sport. This twisting, uncoiling action of the body is also evident in hitting a baseball, or a golf ball. The uncoiling motion is seem in serving a tennis ball or even throwing a forward pass in football or pitching a baseball. The same "snap" at the end that makes a fastball "hop", or a forward pass "spiral" to the receiver, is what's at the end of a properly thrown punch in boxing.

A final thought from a "newbie" in boxing, is that the toughest part to get in shape may actually be the shoulders, because the hardest part of workouts for new boxers is keeping the <u>Hands Up</u> to both defend against and deliver punches. Few other workouts demand such constant shoulder use, strength, flexibility, and endurance.

Discipline

There are many keys to success in both boxing and business—as in learning the correct way to do things. Boxing takes hard work. It requires determination and toughness. So does business—and life. There is another characteristic that both require: discipline. We don't mean discipline in the punitive sense. We mean the discipline to do the right things, in the right ways, at the right times, most or all of the time.

So few people truly have solid discipline. It's so easy to not have it. Leave your home or workplace a little sloppy—poor discipline. Don't keep your hands up in the boxing ring—poor discipline. The biggest difference is that in boxing there is often immediate feedback—you get hit in the face with a punch when you don't keep your hands up.

Stories from the Gym: The Marine and the Lady

One day eight off-duty Marines came into the gym for a little workout. They clearly felt that they were in peak condition and that this was going to be easy. At the same time, one of our regulars, a lady in her mid-fifties came in to workout in the same "class." As the workout proceeded, the Marines were huffing, puffing, grunting and groaning.

(One of the Marines actually had to go outside to vomit, not as unusual as you might think for strenuous workouts, and people who are unprepared for them).

Meanwhile, the mid-fifties lady kept right up with the workout—keeping pace with the remaining seven Marines, a fact we pointed out to them at the end. There is such a thing as being in shape, and an entirely different thing called "being in fighting shape."

Feedback

Like touching a hot stove causes instant feedback, and instant learning, if it sticks in your mind. Training is an important element of discipline, since it attempts to make habits out of the proper behavior. When getting ready to go out in the morning or go to bed at night, such tasks as shaving or doing your hair or brushing your teeth are habitual—almost automatic. In fact, if you vary your routine too much, you might actually forget to do one of them, because you rely on habit to remind you.

The same goes for boxing. If you don't learn that there are two parts to throwing a punch—throwing the punch (correctly) and then getting your hand back up to defend, you will probably get hit a lot while admiring your work (the punch you threw). Footwork works the same way. We mentioned balance. If you are off balance due to bad footwork or the position of your feet, it's a lot easier to get knocked down.

Sayings from the Gym: "Get wrapped up."

(Get your hands wrapped up, ready to put your gloves on)

Habit determines so much of this, and habit is created by training and repetition. In work, there are prescribed ways to do things, and deviating from them usually has adverse consequences. Come in late repeatedly, and there are consequences. Deviate from the prescribed policies, and trouble usually follows. The same is true in life. Drive over the speed limit or roll through stop signs, and sooner or later, there will be consequences. Treat people badly, and they usually reciprocate, and treat you badly.

Sayings from the Gym: "If you have to vomit, go outside!"

(No vomiting allowed in the gym!)

One of the benefits of boxing as a learning tool is that the feedback (after failing to have good discipline) is often immediate, sometimes painful and occasionally devastating (a knock out, in boxing). Learn good discipline, and learn the right ways to do things, and know how the wrong ways are harmful and bad (so you will want to avoid them). Learn from the consequences. Everything you do, in boxing, in work/business and in life, has consequences. Some are good; some are bad. You can learn and choose which kind of outcome you want.

Self-Reliance

You are in that ring all alone with no one else to rely on. The people in your corner can only help you between rounds. The same often applies in life. You can get help later, but you need to decide what to do now! How you do in the ring, how you do in your job, your career and your life, depends on how YOU do.

How confident are you in your ability. Are you willing to take responsibility for the consequences of your actions? Are you willing to learn the habits you need and have the discipline required to do things in the way that gives you the best chance of success? We hope so. To help you with this, the chapters that follow will briefly point out more lessons from boxing that will help plant these points firmly in your mind.

Stories from the Gym: "*It Changes You!*"

A common change we see after people have started coming to the gym is that they are not only getting in better shape physically, but also mentally. Somehow, the workouts in the gym, which involve learning the principles of boxing, and then actually using them (whether on the heavy bag or in the ring) builds confidence and self-assurance. One of the most notable changes happened in "Mike" who changed dramatically. Not only was he more confident and it showed. He also was more relaxed. It's amazing how building competence will to that to a person—for the better!

We will continually emphasize lessons from the "sweet science" of boxing, tough lessons that apply to many different situations. If we are successful, we will have "trained you" (in the boxing vernacular) to be more prepared, more capable, more confident and more self-reliant—and that combination usually means more successful too. Then it is up to you to get in fighting shape, build that strength, flexibility and endurance so that you can persevere and win—at whatever you do.

There is another interesting situation that happens in a boxing gym. It's hard to do common things with your boxing gloves on—like grabbing a water bottle or blowing your nose, or pulling your pants up.

Stories from the Gym: "Keep your pants on"—and don't be afraid to ask for help!"

One day, an exceptionally attractive young woman came into the gym for her lesson/workout. After she was all "gloved up" (had her hands wrapped and her gloves on), she kept bending over stretching and realized that her trunks were a bit loose, and the more times she bent over, the more they crept down, and down, and down—exposing her tattoo, (and dangerously close to exposing more than that.) Finally after several tries with her gloves on, she had to ask for our help pulling her pants up before they got "too far down." (Several of the guys volunteered to help her.) Sometimes it's better to ask for help than to be too self-reliant, when what you are doing is just not working. Ask for help.

Kids Enjoy Boxing Too!

We suspect a lot of people think that the only young folks who are interested in boxing are the "toughs" or the "inner-city kids" that are typically part of the old time boxing gyms. Nothing is further from the truth. Many of the lessons to be learned in a good boxing gym are important life lessons regardless of age. Discipline, hard work, self-control, self-reliance, physical fitness, competition, and many, many more principles come from the gym and influence the lives of young people

Sayings from the Gym: "Let's get ready to have some fun!"

A number of young people—boys and girls—come to the gym to "have fun!" While they are there, they happily decide to do the work outs, learn the principles— and also learn some "self-defense" principles. Nobody better try to "bully" these kids! You see, what is taught in the gym is not just boxing, and what is practiced in the gym is not just fitness or "fighting," it's also that other F word: **fun!**

Stories from the Gym: "*How do you really feel about that?*"

We kind of expected to get some kids who were being bullied coming into the gym to learn how to defend themselves. We do. What we didn't quite expect is how much kids would "open up" and talk to us about all kinds of things.

Sometimes we aren't sure what to do with what they tell us. Our fall back position is often to ask or suggest that they talk to their parents about "whatever it was." At other times, maybe they just need an adult figure to listen to them, care about what they have to say, and act like it.

As Yogi Berra once said, "It's surprising how much you can see by just looking." In our case, "It's surprising how much you can learn by just listening."

There's no doubt that kids gain in self-respect, confidence and maturity as a result of the lessons we try to teach them in the gym. It's great to see them "growing up before your very eyes."

What the Sullivan brothers and their staff teach kids in the gym while they are having fun, is respect, dignity, toughness, and how to be a stronger, better person—and that is something that lasts for a lifetime—inside the gym and outside of it.

So, when you see **kids in the gym** and some of them look pretty young—they are. But if you don't respect them, get in the ring for a little friendly sparring session and you will!

YOU MUST HAVE A PLAN AND FOLLOW IT

"Everybody has a plan until they get hit in the face!

—Mike Tyson

2

YOU MUST HAVE A PLAN

AND FOLLOW IT

You must have a plan...for a fight and for a job, for a business and for your life—and it must be based on SWOT: Strengths, Weaknesses, Opportunities and Threats. Then you must follow that plan as much as possible, but...how?

Strengths and Weaknesses

We all have strengths and weaknesses. Sometimes we know and acknowledge them and at other times we are in denial about what they are. Denial is a dangerous place, because the real world will often "set us straight" and that can be very painful. Thus it is in the boxing ring.

Often fighters compete against weak opposition and build up an impressive record of wins and losses. They might even be undefeated. Nowhere in that array of easy opponents are they forced to face an important fact or two: they have weaknesses that none of these easy opponents have exploited, and these easy wins have not developed their strengths to confirm just how "strong" they are.

In life we might breeze through some easy classes in school, or do very well at a job that is not very hard. The real test comes when we step up a level. Boxing matches usually reveal quickly how prepared—in strengths and weaknesses—an aspiring fighter is when he (or she) steps up a level to tougher competition.

If there was "denial" and those strengths were not all that strong, and the weaknesses were glaring but as yet not exposed, the result is ugly and often humiliating. The jump from easy high school classes to tough college classes can be like this. So can the move from performing well in a good, routine job, to being promoted to one of a supervisor or manager, who must constantly deal with a multitude of unexpected problems for which there is no easy solution.

Stories from the Gym: "Watch out for Ringers"

One of the fairly common occurrences in a boxing gym is that a stranger comes usually with a fit young fellow (or girl) and says they just want to "tap around" a little bit. Frequently they will claim to have little or no experience in boxing. After a short time either in the gym or more often, in the ring, we see them pounding someone, or beating on them. Clearly this person was a "ringer" who wanted someone they could take advantage of (they hoped) to boost their ego, or show good they were, or tough they were against unsuspecting competition. We watch out for these kinds of deceptive people (it's usually the "trainer" more than the fighter), but we are running a boxing gym, so "ringers" occasionally will find their way into our ring.

Sayings from the Gym: "Beware of 'ringers'."

The place to find and expose strengths and weaknesses in boxing is in the gym, not in the ring during a match. The place to do it in business is in training programs, or apprenticeships, or preparatory positions— before making the big jump. In life, there is often no chance to figure out your strengths and weaknesses. There is no manual for how to raise children—and it's worse as they grow up and find new challenges—for which parents are totally unprepared.

There is no easy training program for how to deal with the loss of a job, loss of income, a debilitating illness, or worst of all, the loss of a loved one. In these situations, there is one lesson from the boxing gym that is the best advice: get help!

Find someone who has endured that challenge and survived it. Find a "trainer" who can give help you build the strengths (patience, thinking through problems, feeling OK about asking for help—and where to get it), and over come the weaknesses (that helpless feeling of being clueless about what to do next; that fear that there is 'no way out"— because there usually is).

Ironically, the tough, sometimes brutal sport of boxing offers a couple of simplistic, yet effective lessons to building strengths and overcoming weaknesses. The first is that in boxing when you are getting "beaten up" sometimes the smartest things to do are either "tie the person up" (grab their arms so they can't hit you) or even "take a knee" (kneel down on the canvas and concede a "knockdown") to give you time to get your wits about you.

Much of the preparation for coping with your strengths and weaknesses in life, in work/business and in boxing requires being honest with yourself. Don't kid yourself that things will "somehow fix themselves," because they usually don't. Rely on trained, qualified advisors (in boxing, this is your "corner-man") who can observe what's happening from the relative peace and safety of being "outside the action." A good corner-man can provide encouragement, but also a plan of how to cope with the pressure of being "in the fight." He can also help with one of the most disabling of weaknesses—fear, and one of the most disruptive reactions—panic.

Sayings from the gym: ABC: *"Always Be Cool"*

Calm under pressure is very important—don't panic!

Panic and fear are irrational behaviors, but when you are in a physical confrontation—a fight in the boxing ring—these are not all that unusual. If you have doubts, if you don't believe in yourself and your preparation, then fear creeps in. Then bad things happen and panic about what to do next, follows. The same thing happens in that pressure filled business meeting, that tough discussion with the boss, or when a big problem at home pops up.

Opportunities & Threats

The lesson is that some problems are genuinely unexpected; but most of them are predictable or at least might be expected. Threats are more worrisome, but just as getting ready for a boxing match needs to consider the threats presented by that opponent, so does dealing with work/business or life problems. In boxing, if the opponent is a hard puncher, then extra training on defense against that kind of opponent is in order. If the opponent is wily and fast, or has an exceptionally long reach that requires a different kind of training.

In life some problems are unavoidable, but others can be reduced by discipline and preparation. Do you have a "rainy day fund" to deal with that unexpected financial threat. The car breaks down, or the water heater springs a leak, or there is an unexpected illness, all of which present both psychological and financial threats. The only way to cope with these is through preparation.

In boxing, there is a term "peaking for the fight." That means feeling confident that the training was done properly—physically in fighting shape, technically understanding your strengths and weaknesses and how to compensate for them, knowing the nature of your opponent and what to do to minimize his strengths and threats.

This is little different from preparing for a job interview, for an important meeting in which you must report on progress, or that tough session at school about a misbehaving or underperforming child. (Hopefully not for a meeting with the police or other authorities!) Financial crises will happen—plan on them, and do the best you can to prepare for them. That's why insurance companies exist. That's why it's important to figure out how to build "rainy day funds" even when it's hard to "make ends meet."

Then don't be too proud to ask for help. Everybody needs a good "corner-man"—an adviser for life, a mentor for work, a consultant for business, etc. This kind of "truth teller" is an essential support partner in the boxing ring—and in life. Don't wait; get prepared.

Sayings from the Gym: "I guarantee you'll be a different person in 6 months."

Once you have recognized your strengths and weaknesses and made a plan to deal with the known threats, you need to figure out how to exploit opportunities—because that is your real path to success. In boxing, it can be as simple as observing some trait the opponent has that makes him vulnerable. Does he carry his left hand too low, opening up a spot for a straight right hand lead? Does he always dip or lean over in one direction when throwing a certain punch, opening him up for a counter punch? Or does he simply leave a weak jab out there begging to be countered with a right over the top of it?

In work, business, and life—just like in boxing—the best places to look for opportunities is where you have been successful in the past. Was it in selling or leading people, in making things of offering services, or in helping others? Was it in spending quality time with the family on simple, low cost activities like picnics or going fishing? Or was it in going to school events, or sporting events, or festivals together?

Perhaps it was simply having family meals together, and not making them into "negative" sessions. Focus on what happened that was good, or fun, or funny. (Laughter is an amazing medicine.) Which behaviors and activities and approaches were most effective in seizing the opportunities in the past in your life? Do more of them. Then focus on your dreams and your wishes.

Some boxers can actually imagine the moment of victory, or the time they threw the deciding punch. Visualizing success is a powerful tool—in the ring, or in the real world of life. Now let's get on with more points about succeeding in that "real world" and changing your life.

WHEN REALITY
STRIKES—IT HURTS

"Don't ask why someone keeps hurting you; ask why you keep letting them."

3

WHEN REALITY STRIKES—IT HURTS

In boxing, the bell rings and everything changes. Reality strikes. Get those hands up and keep them up; elbows in too. Someone is out there competing with you, trying to hit you—before you hit him. The ability to adapt to the reality of the fight once it starts will determine whether you survive and win.

While it may not be this brutal in business or in life—it might be after all. Reality in those setting might mean finding yourself in a job you clearly can't handle. Or worse yet, it might mean finding yourself in a relationship (marriage) you should have never gotten into.

Or, another "reality strikes" situation is to be in one of those wonderful relationships, have a good job(s), and maybe be starting a family when the good job(s) disappear and financial hardship follows soon thereafter. When that happens the economic loss is just the first "punch," usually followed soon afterward by marital/relationship troubles—involving money.

How can you prepare for the first few blows (of reality) in the ring, or in life or work? That's hard to do, but the first step in preparation is realizing that it could happen, and maybe will happen to you or friends, family, etc.

This is where the "getting in shape" (physically and fiscally) is important. It's also where having a backup plan of some sort can help a lot. Whether it's in the ring, by tying the opponent up in a clinch, or taking a knee, or in life, where it means having a little rainy day fund built up and another kind of job that you can fall back on.

But if you are not prepared, if you panic, things get worse before they get better. When the pressure is on in the boxing ring, fighters tend to tighten up, which makes them less flexible, less able to throw punches or dodge the ones being thrown at them.

It's really hard not to "tighten up" when things get tough—we know that—but it's important to Always Be Calm (ABC) and in control while you look for alternatives. Sometimes the fear is even worse than the reality—but if you are unprepared—the reality is pretty bad all by itself.

Sayings from the Gym: "When reality strikes, don't panic!"

One of the most humbling, yet important things you might do is the equivalent of "taking a knee"—and that is going to someone close to you and asking for their help—fast. Acting fast when you are in trouble in the boxing ring is really important, because the opponent is "bearing down on you" trying to take advantage of the fact that you are stunned, hurt, confused, and probably afraid.

Life is that way too. Sometimes a good "corner-man" can bring calm and help reduce the fear, so it would smart to think about who might be your "corner-man" in your life or work—a banker, pastor, sibling, parent, or just a close friend—but do it now, don't wait until you are in trouble.

Since there are a lot more life lessons to learn from boxing, let's get on with some of those, next. As you go through the book, you'll find we repeat some points over and over. That's no mistake. It's intentional because with repetition comes retention, which leads to learning. Some experts say you don't really get something until you've heard it six or seven times, but we will try to avoid telling you the same things over and over...if you'll try to remember them the first (or second) time.

Sayings from the Gym: "Hands up!"

PROTECT YOURSELF AT ALL TIMES

"In the end, you have to protect yourself at all times."

—Floyd Mayweather, Jr.

4

PROTECT YOURSELF AT ALL TIMES

One of the first rules when you step into a boxing ring is "Protect yourself at all times." If you watch boxing matches on TV you almost always hear the referee tell this to the fighters in the pre-fight meeting at the center of the ring.

But don't forget that to win a boxing match, you must beat the competitor by hitting them—at the same time that competitor is trying to beat you to the punch and hit you.

In physics one of the rules you learn—called one of the Laws of Physics—is "for every action, there is an equal and opposite reaction." That's definitely true in boxing, and probably true in many other situations in life. Knowing about this "law" at least warns you about what is likely to happen.

Sayings from the Gym: "Protect yourself at all times."
Again! Always!

Ironically, in life and work, one of the most common instances of it is when you get upset or become angry because something isn't going your way. What do you do? You take it out on the person in front of you, whether they caused it or can control it or not. (The same goes for when you are on the phone or emailing or texting.) When that happens, what happens next? Usually that person becomes equally upset with you, which actually reduces your chance of getting what you wanted in the first place. Remember: "action leads to reaction" good or bad.

When you try to impose your will on the opponent in boxing, the normal reaction is the opponent fights back. But boxing is a confrontational sport, so that's appropriate. There are some settings in life and business where you have to try to impose your will in a confrontation, but you might consider going about it differently. That's called "negotiation."

You don't get what you deserve in life; you get what you negotiate and work to get. Even in boxing, negotiation plays an important rule. So does preparation and hard work. How large a ring will there be? What brand and weight of gloves will be used? Even what weight limit will apply for the bout and might that be negotiable? Each such decision can provide an advantage or disadvantage; so "protect yourself at all times."

Another important point that needs to be mentioned here is "momentum." A change in the momentum can change the course of a boxing match and a life or career. Some folks would say, "you're either hot, or you're not." We're not sure that's how it needs to be.

You control a lot of momentum by how you behave and perform. Taking control of things in boxing is often called "ring generalship." It's a big factor in how judges score boxing matches. "Ring generalship" in life can also mean how you try to manage and control what's going on in your life, at your job, or in your career.

Sayings from the Gym: "Fight back!"

(Resist the urge to cover up and get pounded.)

An interesting observation about momentum is that you can usually tell who's winning in most sporting events—boxing included—by watching to see who's attacking and who's defending. The attacker is usually winning because he's dictating the pace of things and the defender is reacting, which results in him being slower to act, and later with punches. The exception to this is the skilled counter-puncher, in boxing, who thrives on reacting to an opponents mistakes and taking advantage of them.

The other point to remember is that in a boxing match, one hard punch can reverse the momentum all at once. This is often true in life, business and a career. A single bold move, if well planned and executed can change everything—reversing momentum in your favor. Making the big deal, getting the big order, or accomplishing the difficult assignment can all be equivalent to that "big punch"—a momentum changer.

Sayings from the Gym: "He hits like a train!"

Footnote: Ring generalship: The ability of a boxer to dictate the pace, style and tactics of a bout vis-a-vis his opponent. According to the 1929 Rules of the New York State Athletic Commission, for example, "ring generalship" comprised "such points as the ability to quickly grasp and take advantage of every opportunity offered, the capacity to cope with all kinds of situations which may arise; to foresee and neutralize an opponent's method of attack; to force an opponent to adopt a style of boxing at which he is not particularly skillful."

THE FEELING OUT PROCESS

(THE JAB)

Everything starts with **the jab.** *It's the most important weapon in a boxer's arsenal. The jab helps to set up your other punches, can distract your opponent, find your range & keep an opponent off you.*

5

THE FEELING OUT PROCESS
(THE JAB)

The jab is a straight punch that is used for setting things up, or just feeling out an opponent. The jab can be both a defensive and an offensive weapon, just like feeling out the market and the competition in business, the jab starts things out. But it is the cross (the straight right cross for a conventional boxer) that is often the deciding punch—and it is set up by a stiff left jab.

The correct way to throw the jab is to rotate your hand as your arm extends from the vertical position (where you were protecting your face with that hand) into the horizontal position—or even a little more, at the end of the punch. This action is like the "snap" referred to earlier from other sports.

Some people think that the twisting action also tends to cut the other fighter if the punch lands just right, but landing the punch with "snap"—a "stiff jab," is the real objective. Like everything in life, there is a right and a wrong way to do it—including throwing a punch.

<u>Sayings from the Gym:</u> "Trust your jab!"

(Overcome hesitance and throw it with confidence)

You might think it's a bit of stretch comparing life or job experiences to punches, but in fact, they have a lot in common. When you enter a new job, meet a new person, or start a new stage of your life, you begin the "feeling out process." Socially, some of the most important situations happen during those "feeling out processes," where neither party knows what to expect from the other. It's the same way in the ring.

Like the jab in boxing, you might be tentative, just pushing yourself out there to see what resistance you find. Or, like a "stiff jab" you might go out there with purpose and more than a little force. Once you see what reaction you get (remember that old action-reaction stuff?), then you decide if you want to do some more feeling out, or move onto something different.

Stories from the Gym

"Getting Past Parental Protection"

This story involves a couple of young people—a boy and a girl. We won't share names in this one, but they will know who they are. The boy really wanted to meet the girl and maybe, even ask her out, or at least spend more time with her "somehow." They were both at that fragile age around 15-16 where "dating" can be a difficult "feeling out process." This process becomes much tougher when one of the parents (usually the girl's father) is very protective.

That was the case this time—and the interaction in the gym—the healthy environment, broke down the barriers. You could have seen the surprise on our faces when the ultra-protective father agreed that the two young people could see more of each other. Perhaps the threats that we teach them to deal with in the gym prepare them— and their parents—for dealing with, and recognizing threats in life. In this case the "threat" became an "opportunity," and the outcome was smiles all around.

If the resistance to your "jab" is weak, then it's time to move forward, stiffen the "jab" and maybe prepare for something harder to come next. If you get smacked with a punch over your lazy jab (figuratively, that is), then maybe you have learned enough about that kind of "feeling out process."

Sticking a lazy jab out there, and leaving it out there too long (before getting that hand back in a defensive position to protect your face) is a lot like deciding to try something, but not really giving it much effort or making much of a commitment. Nothing good comes of half-hearted efforts, whether they are in boxing, in business/work, or in life.

One thing happens when you stick the jab out there in boxing, or "stick yourself out there" in life. You will pretty quickly figure out what has to come next. After all, the purpose of this was to either "feel out" the kind of reaction you would get, or set up several other actions (punches, in boxing) that logically follow a good jab.

If you are right-handed, then you would typically jab with your left hand, reserving your right hand for power punching. When you stick a couple of jabs out there and they are met with the wrong kind of resistance, it's time to throw a "combination"—left jab, right cross.

In boxing, combinations are series of punches thrown in rapid succession before an opponent can recover from one punch; he is being hit with another one—usually from the opposite side. These are sometimes called "the old one-two," referring to the rapid order of the punches.

This principle of combination punching can be very effective in boxing, especially if done quickly and with power behind the punches. In business, combinations are used frequently when launching new products or services. Feel out the market first (jab), then once you know the competitor's reaction, and if it is a weak competitive reaction, follow with a stronger, more direct shot (the right cross). If those two work, and hit home, then it's time for the third punch, the left hook.

If that new job is a sales job, you might already imagine how these combinations compare to the strategy and execution. Make the initial contact; feel out the prospect, and if it seems promising, load up for the next contact. This time, it's the old 1-2; a stiff jab at the target to confirm what the earlier one led to, and the follow up with a powerful shot at getting the deal...which is a good segue to the next chapter.

THE FIRST POWER PUNCH: PUNCH:

THE STRAIGHT RIGHT CROSS

"Heat-seeking missile" is an apt description of Thomas Hearns powerful right"...and a straight line <u>is</u> the shortest distance between two points.

6

THE FIRST POWER PUNCH: THE STRAIGHT RIGHT CROSS

The straight right cross for a conventional (right-handed) boxer is often the deciding punch in a fight. It is thrown with the boxer's dominant hand, and thus can be very powerful. And, as the prior chapter explained, it is often set up by, and follows a stiff left jab. I called it the "straight" right-cross, because there are multiple ways to throw a right cross, but the best one is "straight" at the target (usually the opponent's jaw!)

Like the jab, the correct way to throw the right cross is also to rotate your hand as your arm extends from the vertical position (where you were protecting your face with that hand) into the horizontal position—or even a little more, at the end of the punch. This action is like the "snap" referred to earlier from other sports. The difference is that the right cross is a power punch, so it must be delivered with a considerable amount of body pivot and weight behind it—as if you were trying to punch "through" the opponent.

Sayings from the Gym: *"Punch through it!"*

But why throw it straight? Won't the opponent be looking for that? Sure, but you probably know that the shortest distance between two points is a straight line. (We all learned that at school in geometry class.) Since the straight line is the shortest distance from where you start the right cross to the opponent's jaw, that straight right cross gets the punch there faster than one that must loop around and take a longer path.

Since you should have your right hand up near the right side of your face, to protect yourself from being hit (as you throw the left jab, to set up the right cross), then there is no "windup" necessary, as there might be to throw a looping punch. You just pivot, put your weight behind it and fire your right fist straight at the opponents jaw.

Sayings from the Gym: *"Don't push; punch!"* *(Again— The pushed punch has no "snap" to it, and a lot less impact.)*

It's important to commit to the right cross, throw it hard and make it count. Half-hearted punches (as we noted in the prior chapter) usually result in getting hit with a harder counter-punch. If you throw the right cross straight (and not looping), it gets there faster, and it is easier to put your body weight (the real strength) behind it.

Even if it doesn't hit the target squarely (or at all), if you commit to it and throw it hard, wherever it hits on the opponent—he will know you hit him—even if it is on his/her arm. Sometimes, if the opponent blocks the hard, straight right cross with his glove, it drives the glove back into his face—which is not quite as good as landing a punch, but has a somewhat similar effect.

Sayings from the Gym: "You hit like a girl!"

(Usually directed at those who push their punches with no snap to them.)

There are many other situations in which to throw a hard, straight right cross, like over the opponent's lazy, tentative left jab, or between his upraised hands, or occasionally, as the opening punch instead of the jab (called a "right hand lead," a favorite of Floyd Mayweather Jr.). We are taking the time to describe this punch because it can be the winning punch, the "game changer" that shifts the momentum of the match in your favor, or the one that puts the opponent down on the canvas for the count.

There are lots of lessons about life, work, and business that you can learn from these few paragraphs about the hard, straight right cross. In anything you do, if you hope to be successful, you must commit to it. No half-hearted punches; no half-hearted efforts at a new job, a new promotion, a new marriage, or any one of dozens of other life situations.

Sayings from the Gym: "Commit to your punches if you are going to throw them".

Half-hearted punches usually get countered with stiff ones.

Taking the straight-line, direct path is also a good lesson. Speed is a powerful advantage in almost anything you do. If you can do it faster (and better) than competitors, you win, and they lose. That's why a common phrase used to describe this is "beating them to the punch." Sounds a lot like a boxing term, doesn't it?

Trying hard, committing and putting your body behind whatever you do will also yield results even if you don't hit your target exactly. Just like the hard, straight right cross that only hits the opponent with a glancing blow, a good hard shot at a job, a sale, a promotion, or many other life opportunities, might be enough to succeed, even if it misses a little. Plus, people who are willing to make commitments are typically winners in all walks of life. A wise man once said, "losers make promises, and winners make commitments." Don't make promises you might break. Make commitments you plan to keep.

Even the Star Wars series had something to say about being committed. One of Yoda's famous lines was spoken to Luke Skywalker when he said, *"Alright, I 'll give it a try." Yoda said: "No! Try not. Do... or do not. There is no try."*

Yoda's message was clear, even in his backward way of speaking. Without commitment, there can be no success— there is "no try," there is only "Do, or do not." The same goes for throwing a right cross or succeeding in life or work. Even then, however, timing is important. Choosing the right time to "Do..." is why we opened with the chapter about the jab and the feeling out process.

It's not as simple as just going into a boxing ring and throwing punches. Do that and you will not be so happy with the outcome. If you go all the way back to the chapter about getting in shape and quickly skim forward, you will see that this chapter is just one in series of "Do" steps, and that leads us into the next chapter.

IN CLOSE: DEFENSE & THE PUNCH THEY NEVER SEE COMING

"The punch that puts you to sleep is not so much the hard punch as the punch that you don't see coming..."
—Mohammed Ali

7

IN CLOSE: DEFENSE & THE PUNCH THEY NEVER SEE COMING

Remember the part about "protect yourself at all times?" That means being in shape to do one of the hardest things in boxing–keeping your hands up to protect your head and face, and being ready to move your forearms and elbows around to protect your body and avoid getting hit with punches that come up the middle (like uppercuts).

When you are out in the middle of the boxing ring and can see what the opponent is doing, you will usually (but not always) see punches coming. That gives you a chance to block them and, if you are good enough, to counter-punch. When you get close to the opponent, it opens up opportunities to throw different, but powerful punches–the hook and the uppercut.

The problem is that opportunity also exists for your opponent, and these are punches that can hit you, without you seeing them coming. Punches that hit you when you don't see them are coming, often do the most damage, because you can't "roll with the punch," you can't block or deflect it, and you can't even tighten up your muscles (in your stomach) to withstand them. Ouch. But remember the principle of speed—do it to them before they do it to you—and do it better.

Sayings from the gym: The Golden Rule of Boxing: "It is better to give than to receive!"

The hook and the uppercut are the in-close punches that often seem to "come out of nowhere." Why? Because when two people have their bodies very close to each other, it's hard to see what the opponent's hands are doing.

This happens in business all the time. Competitors launch products and/or marketing/sales offensives that you neither expect nor see coming—and that can knock you off your feet. Sometimes, these will be "knockoffs"—nearly identical copies of your own product or service. Those hurt a lot. At other times, you should expect something to be coming from a competitor because you learned the law about "action and reaction."

With that in mind, consider why the hook and the uppercut are so powerful. They are short punches; no windup. They are thrown with a lot of body involvement, pivoting the body and moving the arm and hand through a very short arc directly from where it was to the part of the opponent's body you are aiming for. The uppercut usually aims for the point of the chin. Hooks can be thrown at either the head or the body, or anywhere in between. Hooks often strike the side of the boxer's head around the ear, and this kind of a blow can disrupt their equilibrium—making it easier to knock them off their feet.

In your life, when someone or something close to you does something to hurt you, it hurts even more than you expect. That's an important lesson from boxing—you probably didn't even see it coming. What can you do? Try to "roll with the blow" literally or figuratively, until you regain your equilibrium and sense of balance.

Sayings from the Gym: "If you can control the action, you have a much better chance of winning."

In the ring, one defensive approach is to push the other boxer away from you, or spin them around, to both buy time, and gain some distance—so you can see what's going on. This is another form of controlling the action—remember the term "ring generalship." This sometimes happens in life when someone close to you does something unexpected and hurtful. You push them away, get some distance, and buy some time to figure out what just happened. Then you can regain your bearings and figure out what to do next.

When the two fighters are in a "clinch" (holding each others arms to their body), sometimes one of the fighters' hands will come free. He can continue punching with that free hand until the referee breaks up the clinch. That's "sort of" within the rules. (You can't hold and hit...but if you are being held and have a hand free, you can keep hitting until the referee breaks you apart.

In business, that kind of situation sometimes occurs. You think you have tied up the competitor with some move you made, only to discover that he had "one hand free" and was still doing damage. Always make sure you take into account both hands, and yes, you guessed it: Protect yourself at all times!

TO GET A BREAK, GRAB THE OPPONENT & "TIE THEM UP"

"It's hard for someone to hit you when you're hugging them."

—George Foreman

8

TO GET A BREAK, GRAB THE OPPONENT & "TIE THEM UP"

When you are under attack, don't be afraid to tie up the other guy. This can be a great defensive move, but it's also one that can lead to a different kind of strategy. One of former heavyweight champ George Foreman's favorite lines was, "It's hard for them to hit you when you are hugging them." Foreman should know about defensive tactics having been on the receiving end of one of the wiliest tactics ever used.

Sayings from the Gym: "Tie 'em up!"

Take a break, to use the opponent's energy, grab their arms under yours.

An aging Muhammad Ali fought the much younger and stronger George Foreman on October 30, 1974, in Zaire (now the Congo) in the now famous "Rumble in the Jungle." Ali used what he called a "Rope-A-Dope" tactic, in which he covered up his face and body with his hands and elbows, leaned back against the ropes and allowed the stronger George Foreman to wear himself out in the heat and humidity, pounding away to no avail, while Ali simply blocked punch after punch.   After seven rounds, Ali came out of his turtle-like shell, and began punching the tired Foreman, knocking him out in the eighth round in a huge upset.

Not too many years later, Foreman retired from boxing, only to come back when he was well into his forties, a much smarter fighter, still strong and powerful. It was in this era that he learned and extolled the virtue of "hugging an opponent" to avoid being hit.

Every boxer gets tired as a match wears on. Even the best-conditioned boxers lose either some speed or some power on their punches.   When they get in a little trouble, or even if there is no trouble, but they need a little break, they can take a brief rest by clinching, tying up the opponents arms. This gives them a chance to refresh, regroup and get on with doing better things.

It's surprising how many people in life or work suffer from some form of "burnout." This can be a very serious problem, affecting their physical and mental health and well-being. Today's always-on society, with cell phones and mobile devices tracking us everywhere, makes it tough to take a break, to go "into a clinch or tie someone up," figuratively speaking. Yet that is often exactly you need to do at times. Hug somebody!

Sayings from the Gym: "She looks like she has issues."

A woman that has tunnel vision, angrily taking out her gloves on the heavy bag.)

Vacations are not even as restful as they used to be—if you even take one. It takes a day or two just to "decouple" from the pressure of the work (like a fight). Then, if there is a constant barrage of interruptions from the office, the job, the family, etc. and problems to be dealt with—there is no real rest at all.

Everyone needs to "recharge his or her batteries" and take time to "refocus on what you are trying to achieve." One of the best statements says, "Too often we struggle to climb the ladder of success, never bothering to stop and see if it is leaning against the right wall." How true.

In a boxing match, and in life, it is sometimes wiser to temporarily "throw in the towel," another boxing term widely used to signify giving up on the challenge at hand.

There are times when it is better to "live to fight another day," instead of trying to go on when you are clearly beaten and exhausted. Stop. Regroup and recharge. Take a fresh look at things—you might see a whole new way to win.

Stories from the Gym

"We are not 'shrinks,' but we do a lot of therapy in the gym."

We figured that if people started coming around regularly, we'd get to know them pretty well. We just never imagined how that might turn out. Sometimes all a person needs is a "willing and sympathetic ear"—someone to listen to his or her issues or troubles. At other times, solutions are so obvious they should see them (and actually do, but can't admit it). In these cases they just need someone to tell them the obvious—or encourage them to "just do the right thing!" That's why we say, "we do a lot of therapy in the gym." Sometimes they are not so much boxing classes as therapy classes. And they can take out any pent up aggression on the heavy bag while they are at it.

LEARN, ADJUST, ADAPT AND CHANGE

"It is not the strongest or the most intelligent who will survive but those who can best manage change."

—Charles Darwin

9

LEARN, ADJUST, ADAPT AND CHANGE

There are very few boxers who can change their entire approach and plan in the middle of a match. Some of the great ones can—and did—Sugar Ray Robinson, Sugar Ray Leonard, Muhammad Ali, Marvin Hagler, Bernard Hopkins, Roy Jones Jr., and Floyd Mayweather Jr.

As the fight goes on, the plan of attack must continually be evaluated, adjusted and refined—in business and in boxing. But, that's hard to do in the middle of the battle. Conditions change. You both tire. You learn new information: what to watch out for, and "what works—what doesn't—and why." (That's another entire book in itself.)

Big advantages can be gained by making adjustments that stay within the framework of what you planned to do, but improve on it slightly. The problem is that this is very difficult to do.

Boxing, like most other human activities, depends on learned ways of doing things, and of reacting to other things. When the action is fast, these behaviors must happen in split seconds. That's how trainers develop fighters. If he does this, you do that. When this happens, you do this. But these kind of plans always are developed in a framework built around the strengths and weaknesses of the boxer (remember SWOT?)

Sayings from the Gym: "You are taking it to a new level."

When someone improves so much that everyone notices.

If a boxer is fast, one strategy is employed; if he is slower, but has a powerful punch, a different one is used. If a fighter is best as a "boxer" (skillful at moving about, punching rapidly, and using a wide variety of punches) then a good plan is to capitalize on that skill.

If a fighter is a "puncher" (throwing hard punches, but from fewer different positions and in carefully planned situations), yet a different fight plan is used. Some fighters claim to be good at both (a "boxer-puncher"), but in the heat of the fight, are almost always better at one or the other. It is that skill/habit they revert to under pressure. This is a natural human tendency.

The same happens to us in work, in life, and everywhere else. We like to do what we are good at, and we become better at doing what we like to do—and vice versa. Many job situations involve promotions that move someone who was good at doing something into a job where they no longer do it. Now they must rely on others to do it—and direct their efforts. This is a very different situation, which can transform a valuable employee into an inept one—through no fault of his/her own.

Many life situations seem to always develop the same way, especially arguments at home, with family members. Some little upset starts things off, and then they quickly revert to the same old, same old argument about money, personal habits, long-standing gripes or differences of opinion. Changing and breaking these habitual ways is as hard as a boxer trying to become a puncher (or vice versa) in the middle of a fight.

The solution lies in trying to unravel the nature of the problem, and realizing that it almost always comes back to the same problems. The same occurs in the boxing ring. The puncher will be too slow to become a boxer and the boxer lacks the power to become a puncher. The challenge is to become the best possible version of what they are good at doing—not something different. And don't try to change in the middle of the fight.

Finally, there is the one thing that happens eventually to most boxers. They get knocked out—unconscious. This is a traumatic event, which can change their entire outlook on boxing. Some consciously decide they just don't want to fight any more. Others don't admit it, but the fear and uncertainty, and the memory of that event, remains in them and hampers their progress. Still others get over it. They recognize that this is one of the risks of the sport and decide to continue, but do their best to avoid it in the future.

The equivalent to a knockout in life, or in work is getting fired—and worst of all—when it comes unexpectedly (Like a punch they didn't see coming). Almost equally bad is getting fired "in a bad way," which leaves the person with a damaged psyche—like the boxer that can't get over the knockout.

This is why people who get fired need to get their head around it and decide if they can get over it alone—or if they need help reconciling their sense of self worth with such an event. Too many people just try to go on, but like that boxer who got knocked out, they can't get over it.

Everybody needs help at times. Get help; accept the help; it's a sign of strength, not weakness. The person helping you will appreciate that feeling of being able to help too.

DON'T GIVE UP
DON'T BACK DOWN

"Never give in, never give in, never, never, never, never—in nothing, great or small..."
—Sir Winston Churchill

10

DON'T GIVE UP

DON'T BACK DOWN

In boxing, and in life, the prize goes to the person who outlasts competition. Or perhaps it goes the person who is best prepared, and out works the competition. Or just maybe it goes to the person who has a better plan to use their strengths and avoid their weaknesses, and thus outsmarts the competition. In other words, there are a lot of ways to win.

Sayings from the Gym: "Go, go, go, you can do it!"
(Don't quit fighting; don't quit trying.)

The common denominator is to persist. Don't give up; don't back down. Enough endurance, relentless intensity, mental and physical toughness, and more... can break the spirit of a competitor. You will get hit—the key is how you handle those hits—and how you can recover from them and hit the opponent back. Sometimes it is as simple as imposing your will on a competitor and in the process breaking his/her will down.

It takes courage to persist in the face of adversity. In boxing, one of the scary things that can happen is to get a bad cut on the face, especially around the eyes. The sheer sight of your own blood streaming down, blurring your vision is pretty scary. Another is to get a punch in the nose that is so hard you get a broken nose. The pain is terrific and then there is the added problem of difficulty breathing, and also seeing your own blood again, having it run down your throat and into your stomach.... well, you get it. It's hard.

**Sayings from the Gym:** _"There's no blood in the ring..."(Keep on fighting, nobody's bleeding—yet!)_

But life is hard too. Loved ones get sick. People lose their jobs and don't know how they will get by. Children run around with the wrong crowd and get into some very dangerous and possibly life altering situations. It's not quite the same as a cut, a broken nose and seeing your own blood flowing—but sometimes it can be far, far worse and last much longer.

Toughness is a recurring theme in this book. Boxing demands it and life requires it. There is no magic pill that delivers it. It comes from within a person. Some folks would say it is passed down generation to generation, but I'm not so sure that's true. No doubt the way parents raise children can improve their "toughness." Discipline, which was emphasized earlier as being so important, often comes from upbringing. Disciplinary behavior of parents and in the home also matters. It can be good, bad or unevenly applied.   But all-in-all, tough love is far better than no love at all.

Sayings from the Gym: "You can do it!"

(Encouragement is important.)

When one of those "crushing events"—an injury (in boxing or not), a serious illness, or in the extreme case the loss of a loved one hits you—there is no easy way to deal with it. It just requires an internal strength and toughness (that word again) to get through it.

Sometimes in the boxing ring, a particularly brutal beating will cause someone to "give it up." That just means that the risk, the pain and suffering and the punishment were not worth the expected rewards for continuing.

Some people are just not cut out for the rigors of boxing. Some people are just not cut out for the sacrifices life demands of them either. Whenever we hear that everyone should go to college, we wonder—is that really so?

Not everyone is cut out for college either. There is a great need for tradespeople with skills they learned, to keep our machinery running. There is a great need for people to build roads and houses and commercial buildings, and most of those jobs would benefit little from a college education.

Sayings from the Gym: "Who pissed you off?"

(To a trainer who's in a bad mood, pushing really hard.)

What they would benefit from is the discipline to show up at work every day, on time, and to do a good day's work, something they can be proud of. In many respects the same can be said of a boxing match. In every match there is one winner and one loser—but that doesn't mean the loser is really a "loser." It just means that other person, on that day was better, stronger, more talented, better trained, had more toughness or more endurance, and on, and on.

Perhaps the best aspect of getting in shape for boxing—fighting shape—is to realize how tough it can be, just like life. It prepares you in a very different way, with the confidence to face adversity and get though it—and come out on top. And that leads us to the next chapter—about confidence.

IT'S ALL ABOUT CONFIDENCE & COMMITMENT

Did you hear what this idiot just said? He said it's not about the W! It's everything about the W with me!"
—Bernard Hopkins

11

IT'S ALL ABOUT CONFIDENCE & COMMITMENT

For ten chapters, we have been comparing what it takes to succeed in boxing, in business and in life. There is one more big, important factor to mention here in the middle of the "championship chapters" (like championship rounds 10, 11, and 12 at the end of a fight.)

Confidence—not the kind you talk about—the kind you feel deep down, when the challenge is facing you. Remember this famous saying from the gym, early in the book:

Sayings from the Gym*: "Everybody has a plan until they get hit in the face! —Mike Tyson, former heavyweight champion.*

If you don't have, or can't build confidence, then sit down and have a talk with yourself. Do not step in the boxing ring for any serious fighting. Do not step up for that big promotion at work. And do not expect to go through life making excuses or blaming someone else.

You either believe in yourself or you don't. That doesn't mean you can't learn to believe in yourself. That can be built up like muscle and calluses by enduring and getting through the tough times in whatever you do. What this does mean is that you need to think about, carefully consider and really truly understand what confidence feels like.

Sayings from the Gym: "Make sure you know what you are trying to do then commit to doing it."

This doesn't mean you won't be nervous or have butterflies before a big event—a fight, a meeting at work, a big presentation or a major life event (getting married, for example). Someone once said, *"Confidence is the feeling you have just before you realize what you committed to do."* We've seen people come to the gym who talk a big game; who strut and pose and gesture as if they are filled with confidence. Those are tipoffs that this kind of person isn't truly confident.

Watch a person who comes in to the gym (or the job) quietly and goes about doing the job—whether its boxing or leading a project at work, or being a "stand-up" Dad (or Mom) for the family when times are tough. Confident people don't have to talk about it. They have it— and it shows—if you know what to look for.

A boxer who acts like a punch doesn't hurt, smiling and gesturing, is showing that his (or her) confidence is shaken. A confident fighter works to shake off the effect of the punch, cover up so he doesn't take another one like that and learn to keep his "Hands Up" (and elbows in—those body punches hurt too.)

In boxing the term "bringing a fighter along" refers to the practice of taking fights that will be progressively more difficult, against more talented opponents. The purpose is to gain experience, which is a key part of building confidence.

After winning against a tough opponent, a boxer will have more confidence against the next tough opponent. The same happens in all kinds of sport (races, etc.) and in life. Public speaking terrifies some people, but some jobs demand it. Only after doing it several times, successfully, does confidence begin to build.

Sayings from the Gym: Confidence: "I'm so fast that last night I turned off the light switch in my hotel room and was in bed before the room was dark!" —Muhammad Ali

The same is true in boxing. Fight a tough opponent and win, and confidence soars. This is a big reason boxers talk about "fighting anybody, anytime," right after a good win. There is also the problem of a crushing loss, to someone you expected to and/or should have defeated.

Rebuilding confidence is hard and takes longer, but it is not impossible. Figure out what went wrong, and face facts—was the other guy just better? Or did you not keep your Hands Up and get hit with a "lucky punch?" If so, you must work on how you can do better. It's like a kids game of leapfrog, taking turns jumping over each other, until one of you can't anymore.

The last part of confidence is what's often called toughness or "heart." If a fighter is deeply confident in his ability to win, he will keep fighting and endure. This happens in work or business too. Lose the big order or customer? Don't give up. If you are confident you have what is needed, keep fighting. The loss is only a temporary setback. Commitment is another part of being a winner.

Confidence builds commitment and commitment can build confidence. Announcers often comment on "how bad a fighter wants it" (the win). This combination of confidence and commitment is what carries a fighter through the late rounds when they are fatigued more than imaginable. Watch a fighter's hands drop as the fight wears on. That's why this book's title, "Hands Up," refers to one of the most difficult things to do in boxing—keep your hands up—in position to defend and/or to hit back.

Sayings from the Gym: "Touch gloves and come out fighting."

Do you have the will to win? In anything you do, that is essential. Without the will to win, it's too easy to give up when things get tough. Never give up; never back down. Build confidence and make a commitment—to win.

But remember, in every fight there is a winner and a loser. The fight goes on until the final bell—or someone surrenders. Losing doesn't mean quitting or even being inferior. It just means losing that time, to that person.

Where confidence makes the difference is in understanding and accepting why the loss—and then doing something to become better—and believe you can and will do that. Bring that will to win the next time, and the time after that.

Check the list of great all-time fighters and see how few retired unbeaten over a long (10+year) career. (Nearly none: Rocky Marciano and Floyd Mayweather) It's how a fighter (or a business person, or a family member) comes back from a loss and regains the confidence to go on, being a winner and a champion. Some boxing trainers even think an early loss is good for a fighter. It makes them realize that they aren't invincible, but that they can recover from it and still be successful.

Boxing is a fight. In work it's a job. In life it might be raising children. If the reward is worth the hard work, dedication, risk and sacrifice, you need to "go for it." If you have doubts about your ability to succeed, then you lack confidence, or your confidence is wavering—or you are not committed.

We've emphasized over and over that commitment —the "will to win"—is vitally important. So is the confidence (and courage) to get back up after you've been knocked down and then commit to become better than you were before.

Sayings from the Gym: **_"When you get knocked down, get back up, and keep on fighting."_**

"Going one more round when you don't think you can—that's what makes all the difference in your life."

—Sylvester Stallone ("Rocky")

"YOU AIN'T DEAD YET...IS YOU?"

You are never too old to set another goal or to dream a new dream.
−C. S. Lewis

12

"YOU AIN'T DEAD YET...IS YOU?"

Here we are, at the final, twelfth round. This is it. The end. The conclusion: It's not necessarily who's best that wins. It's who's best prepared, who competes the hardest, who perseveres the most intensely, who understands the nuances of the competition, and who is in the best shape—fighting shape—and has the most will to win.

Playwright George Bernard Shaw once said, *"The strongest, fiercest force in nature is human will."* He was right. The victory goes to the person who is most committed, and proves it by their preparation, intensity, determination, discipline, and will to win. That applies in every sport, certainly in boxing, and in every walk of life.

The title of this chapter was a statement by an old boxer, counseling one of the authors on his philosophy to never give up. He said simply, "You ain't dead yet, is you?"

What will you do now? Will you change your life based on any of the stories, lessons and facts you've learned from this little book. We certainly hope so.

We hope you are thinking about how you might change your life for the better.

We hope you can use the wisdom from the boxing ring and the gym to help you.

We hope the mere fact that you have read this far, and thought about what we have been saying in here will convince you that YOU can determine the outcome of your life.

If you believe those statements and answer this question:

What will you do differently because you know this?

Now get out there and get started—the "bell just rang! Remember, "... It's about changing your life."

EPILOGUE:

"SOMETIMES A FIGHTER GETS OLD FAST"

"I am an old man, I just happen to be an old man that can fight."

—Bernard Hopkins

13

EPILOGUE:

"SOMETIMES A FIGHTER GETS OLD FAST"

A back problem forced me to leave the gym at age 73. It was a few years after that, while <u>Hands Up</u> was being finished that the pressures of a competitive blitz forced the Sullivan Brothers to close the boxing gym. Although they had weathered the economic downturn, they had also ushered in a new era when boxing training was "discovered" as a powerful fitness approach.

Shortly after that scores of new boxing gyms, many with franchises (e.g., Title Boxing), surrounded the Sullivan Brothers gym and blitzed their markets with advertising and loss leader promotional offers. As membership began to decline and still more new gyms closed in (the nearest one less than ¼ mile away), Tim and John decided that it was time to "hang up their gloves" and move on.

Theirs was a valiant effort, which proved that a couple of dedicated guys can launch a business and be at the forefront of a trend. Just as an older fighter wears down as the rounds go by, the pressures became too great to bear, and the Sullivan corner wisely threw in the towel. No matter that the new upstarts won this fight, the old timers proved that the lessons learned in boxing are truly timeless and can be applied to almost everything in life—and especially the world of work, career, and business.

Can you hear the crowd cheering as the final bell sounds, and the decision is rendered? I can! As the competitors make their way proudly to the locker room, the crowd's cheers get louder and louder, and these valiant warriors walk out on their own two feet, heads held high. I wish them health and happiness.

John Mariotti

John Sullivan, John Mariotti, Tim Sullivan

"I'm a dreamer. I have to dream and reach for the stars, and if I miss a star, I grab a handful of clouds."
—Mike Tyson

ALL TIME GREATS IN BOXING

Chronological Order of Career Start Year

<u>Boxer, Career, Record, W-L, KO & %KO</u>

Jack Johnson,	1897-1932, 73-13, 46KO-63%
Benny Leonard,	1911-1932, 85-5, 69KO-81%
Jack Dempsey,	1914-1927, 66-6, 50KO-76%
Gene Tunney,	1915-1928, 61-1, 40KO-66%
Henry Armstrong,	1931-1945, 150-21, 100KO-67%
Marcel Cerdan,	1934-1949, 111-4, 66KO-57%
Joe Louis,	1934-1951, 68-3, 54KO-79%
Archie Moore,	1938-1963, 183-**24**, 136KO-74%
Sugar Ray Robinson,	1940-1965, 173-19, **109KO**-63%
Willie Pep,	1940-1966, **229**-11, 65KO-28%
Jake Lamotta,	1941-1954, 83-19, 30KO-36%
*Rocky Marciano,	**1948-1955, 49-0, 43KO-88%**
Muhammad Ali,	1960-1981, 56-5, 37KO-66%
Carlos Monzon,	1963-1977, 87-3-9, 59KO-59%
Joe Frazier,	1965-1981, 32-4, 27KO-84%
Roberto Duran,	1968-2001, 103-16, 70KO-68%
George Foreman,	1969-1997, 76-5, 68KO-**89%**
Marvin Hagler,	1973-1987, 62-3, 52KO-80
Sugar Ray Leonard,	1977-1997, 36-3, 25KO-69%
Tommy Hearns,	1977-2006, 61-5, 48KO-72%
Michael Spinks,	1977-1988, 31-1, 21KO-66%
Julio Cesar Chavez,	1980-2005, 107-6, 80KO-75%
Evander Holyfield	1984-2011, 44-10, 29KO-53%
Mike Tyson,	1985-2005, 50-6, 44KO-72%
Bernard Hopkins,	1988-2016, 55-8, 32KO-60%
Lennox Lewis	1989-2003, 41-2, 32KO-74%
Roy Jones, Jr.,	1989-2015, 55-8, 40KO-73%
Oscar De La Hoya	1992-2008, 39-6, 30KO-75%
*Floyd Mayweather Jr.	**1996-2017, 50-0, 26KO-65%**
Wladimir Klitschko	1996-2017, 64-5, 53KO-77%

Manny Pacquiao	1995--, 57-6, 38KO-58%
Andre Ward	2004--, 32-0, 16KO-50%
Saul Alvarez	2005--, 49-1, 34KO-68%
Gennady Golovkin	2006--, 37-0, 33KO-**89%**
Mikey Garcia	2006--, 37-0, 30KO-81%
Terence Crawford	2008--, 32-0, 23KO-72%
Sergey Kovalev	2008--, 30-2, 26KO-81%

Many more will follow, but only after a decade-long (or more) reign, does a boxer qualify for these elite ranks.

67927667R00065

Made in the USA
Lexington, KY
26 September 2017